INSIDE THE NFL

AFC NORTH

BY JAMES BUCKLEY JR.

LIBRARY OF CONGRESS CATALOGING-IN-PUBLICATION DATA

Buckley, James, 1963–
   AFC North / by James Buckley, Jr.
      p. cm. – (Inside the NFL)
   Includes index.
   ISBN 1-59296-509-1 (library bound : alk. paper) 1. National Football
League–History–Juvenile literature. 2. Football–United States–History–Juvenile
literature. I. Title: American Football Conference North. II. Title. III. Child's World
of sports. Inside the NFL.
   GV955.5.N35B15 2006
   796.332'64'0973–dc22   2005004808

ACKNOWLEDGEMENTS

The Child's World®: Mary Berendes, Publishing Director

Editorial Directions, Inc.: Russell Primm, Editorial Director and Line Editor; Matt
Messbarger, Project Editor; Elizabeth K. Martin, Assistant Editor; Olivia Nellums,
Editorial Assistant; Susan Hindman, Copy Editor; Susan Ashley, Beth Franken,
Proofreaders; Kevin Cunningham, Fact Checker; Tim Griffin/IndexServ, Indexer;
James Buckley Jr., Photo Researcher and Selector

The Design Lab: Kathleen Petelinsek, Design and Page Production

Photos: Cover: Keith Srakocic/AP
AP/Wide World: 30, 38; Brian Bahr/Getty: 32; David Bergman/Corbis: 2;
Corbis: 25, 26, 27, 28; Focus on Sport/Getty: 36; Tom Hauck/Getty: 11; Jeff
Haynes/Getty: 12; Craig Jones/Getty: 10; Andy Lyons/Getty: 1, 22, 23; Wally
McNamee/Corbis: 18; Doug Pensinger/Getty: 7, 14; Mike Powell/Getty: 21;
Sports Gallery/Al Messerschmidt: 8, 16, 17, 34, 35, 37; Rick Stewart/Getty: 41.

TABLE OF CONTENTS

Published in the United States of America by
The Child's World® • PO Box 326
Chanhassen, MN 55317-0326
800-599-READ • www.childsworld.com

The
**Child's
World**

INTRODUCTION

BALTIMORE RAVENS

Year Founded: 1996

**Home Stadium:
M&T Bank Stadium**

**Year Stadium
Opened: 1998**

**Team Colors: Black,
purple, and gold**

**CINCINNATI
BENGALS**

Year Founded: 1968

**Home Stadium: Paul
Brown Stadium**

**Year Stadium
Opened: 2000**

**Team Colors:
Orange and black**

In 2002, the National Football League (NFL) changed the way its teams are organized. The league moved from six **divisions** of five to six teams to eight divisions of four teams each. One of these new divisions was the AFC (American Football Conference) North, which features some of the NFL's most historic teams. (Most of the teams in the AFC North were formerly part of the AFC Central.) The AFC North also features some of the most confusing city-switching in sports history. We'll see if we can explain it all.

The oldest team in the division is the Pittsburgh Steelers, founded in 1933. They have stayed in Pittsburgh ever since and are the most **stable** team in the division. The Cincinnati Bengals have also remained in the same city since their founding, which was in 1968. Here's where it gets a bit confusing. The founding owner and coach of the Bengals was Paul Brown, who earlier had been the longtime coach of the Cleveland Browns.

The Cleveland Browns were not originally in the NFL at all. From 1946 to 1949, the team played in a short-lived pro league called the All-America Football Conference (AAFC). The Browns joined the NFL in 1950, and Paul Brown coached them to several NFL titles. However, in 1995, the team's owner moved the Browns to Baltimore to become the Ravens. The Ravens are now also in the AFC North.

Meanwhile, fans in Cleveland missed their team enormously. They pretty much forced the NFL to put another team in Cleveland, named (you guessed it) the Browns.

So the AFC North has one team that is the Browns and one team that used to be the Browns. Plus, it has one team founded by a guy named Brown. It's lucky the Steelers have stayed put, or this would really be hard to follow.

The Ravens are the only team in the division with a recent **Super Bowl** title. Baltimore won Super Bowl XXXV over the New York Giants. The Steelers, however, were riding high early in the 2000s, with two AFC Championship Game appearances. Their 15–1 regular season record in 2004 was the best in the league and tied for second best of all time.

But championships or not, it will all become much clearer as you read about these four teams, who between them have racked up a total of nine NFL championships.

CLEVELAND BROWNS

Year Founded: 1946*

Home Stadium: Cleveland Browns Stadium

Year Stadium Opened: 1999

Team Colors: Orange and brown

* Played first four seasons in AAFC.

PITTSBURGH STEELERS

Year Founded: 1933

Home Stadium: Heinz Field

Year Stadium Opened: 2001

Team Colors: Black and gold

CHAPTER ONE

THE BALTIMORE RAVENS

Although the old Cleveland Browns moved to Baltimore in 1995 to become the Ravens, the NFL treats the Ravens as a new team. The history of the Browns remains with the new Browns team (see Chapter Three).

The fans in Baltimore were used to seeing NFL football. From 1953 to 1983, the Colts played there and became an important part of the city. After they moved to Indianapolis, fans desperately wished for a new team. Finally, in 1995, they got their wish. Cleveland Browns owner Art Modell decided to move his team to Baltimore. One of the reasons was that Baltimore promised to build Modell's team a new stadium.

Longtime Colts fans were at first angry that their team was an "old" one from another city. But they soon warmed to the idea, and the team became popular.

The first thing Modell needed was a name for his new team. The NFL decided that the name Browns would remain in Cleveland. A new Browns team would begin playing in 1999. Back in Baltimore, thousands of fans voted, and the winning name was Ravens. The

Pro Bowl passer Vinny Testaverde was a bright spot in the Ravens' first seasons.

name comes from a poem by Baltimore-born poet Edgar Allan Poe. He wrote a famous poem in 1845 called "The Raven."

As with most new teams, the Ravens struggled in their early years. They had a losing record in each of their first three seasons (1996–1998). A highlight for the team was the play of quarterback Vinny Testaverde. He was named to the **Pro Bowl** in 1996.

The Ravens boast not one, but three mascots. Edgar, Allan, and Poe are oversized Ravens who entertain and hang out with fans at games and other events.

Ravens fans enjoy games in a very new stadium.

Another big highlight came in 1998 when the team's new stadium opened. At first, it was called PsiNet Stadium after an Internet company. (The stadium is now called M&T Bank Stadium.)

The Ravens' first coach was Ted Marchibroda, who had coached the Colts from 1975 to 1979, when that franchise was in Baltimore.

After finishing 6–10 in 1998, coach Ted Marchibroda was fired. The new coach was an offensive-minded coach named Brian Billick. This would prove to be Modell's smartest move since packing up for Baltimore.

In Billick's first season, 1999, the Ravens began to show sparks of success. Their powerful defense, led by linebacker Ray Lewis, allowed the third-fewest points in the NFC. Billick didn't make the offense into a powerhouse, but it was very much improved, and the team finished 8–8.

In 2000, the Ravens flew higher than ever before. While helping the team to a 12–4 record, the Lewis-led defense was positively stifling. The defense allowed only 165 points, the fewest ever in a 16-game season. (NFL teams played 14 games in a season until 1977.) They shut out four teams, and they held seven other teams to 10 points or fewer.

"You don't know until you play us," Lewis said. "But our defense is like running into a buzz saw!"

The Ravens' offense that season was led by

Kicker Matt Stover kicked 35 field goals in 2000.

Linebacker Ray Lewis was named the Most Valuable Player (MVP) in the Ravens' Super Bowl XXXV victory.

running back Jamal Lewis. He set a team record with 1,364 rushing yards, while scoring six touchdowns. A key part of their success was also the kicking game. All-Pro kicker Matt Stover led the AFL with 135 points, including 35 field goals, while Jermaine Lewis was a top punt returner.

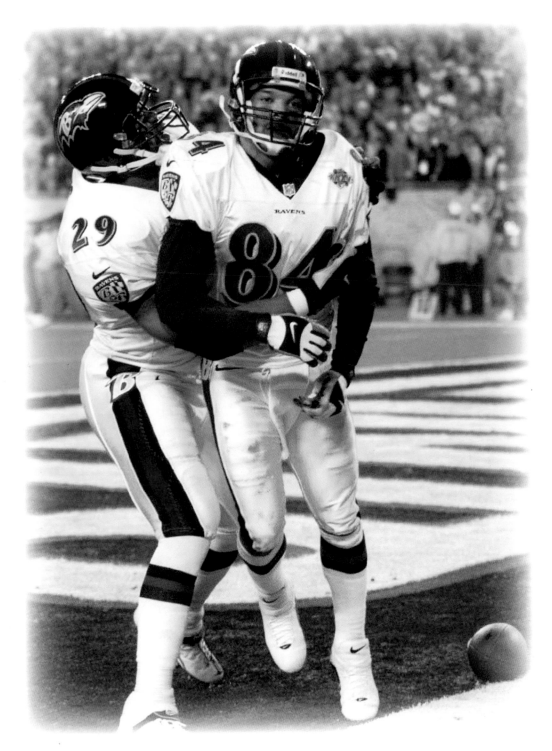

Jermaine Lewis celebrates after scoring on a kickoff return in Super Bowl XXXV.

Fans surrounded Ray Lewis after he was named MVP of the Ravens' Super Bowl victory.

Players and coaches entertain young fans from the Baltimore area at the annual Ravens Rally for Kids.

The Ravens' defense led the way in the playoffs. Against Denver, Jamal Lewis scored twice and the defense held the Broncos to a field goal. Ravens 21, Broncos 3. Facing division rival Tennessee next, Baltimore got help from all its parts. Jamal Lewis scored again, and Stover kicked a field goal. Anthony Mitchell returned a blocked field goal for another score, while Ray Lewis returned an **interception** 50 yards for a touchdown. Ravens 24, Titans 10.

In the AFC Championship Game, veteran tight end Shannon Sharpe scored on a spectacular 96-yard reception from quarterback Trent Dilfer. Stover made three more field goals. And the defense was superb again: The Oakland Raiders managed only one field goal. Ravens 16, Raiders 3. Next stop: the Super Bowl, against the NFC-champion New York Giants!

As they had all season, every part of the Ravens took the team to success. The defense led the way, allowing only 152 yards and no points. Baltimore intercepted four passes, with Duane Starks taking one in for a touchdown. Jermaine Lewis had a marvelous 84-yard kickoff-return score. Dilfer had a touchdown pass, while Jamal Lewis ran for a score. The Giants scored only on a kickoff return; otherwise, they came up empty. Ravens 34, Giants 7. And Baltimore, once home to the NFL-champion Colts, was once again home to football's number-one team.

Baltimore football fans today are thrilled that they now have a team to follow. Their hopes for a football future flew back into town in 1996 on the wings of a raven. Four years later, that Raven was clutching the Vince Lombardi Trophy.

That Super Bowl season kicked off a great run for the Ravens. They returned to the playoffs three times in the next four seasons, plus they won a division championship in 2003. Defense remains the bedrock of the Ravens team. Ray Lewis was joined by fellow linebacker Peter Boulware, safety Ed Reed, and sack-happy defensive

> The Ravens tied a dubious NFL record by going five consecutive games without a touchdown in 2000. Still, their defense was so dominant that they won two of those games.

Kyle Boller took over as the Ravens' starter in 2003.

Ravens coach
Brian Billick was
an assistant director
of public relations
for the San
Francisco 49ers
from 1979 to 1980.

lineman Terrell Suggs. Reed's nine interceptions led the NFL in 2004.

On offense, the key player was quarterback Kyle Boller. He was drafted by the Ravens in the first round of the 2003 draft and quickly became the team's starter. He combined with Jamal Lewis to carry the Ravens to two winning seasons.

CHAPTER TWO

THE CINCINNATI BENGALS

The story of the Bengals is like a roller coaster—
the team has reached some terrific heights. But
they have also plunged to some depressing depths. At
times, they have been among football's best teams.
More recently, they have been among the least
successful.

The roller-coaster ride began in 1968 when
legendary coach Paul Brown fielded the first Bengals
team. Brown was one of the NFL's greatest all-time coaches (see
Chapter Three). He would not have as much success with Cincinnati,
however, but his reputation helped the team get started.

Cincinnati played its first two seasons in the American Football League (AFL). The AFL merged with the NFL in 1970, and the
Bengals joined the AFC Central Division. They quickly made their
mark by finishing the season with seven victories in a row. Their
8–6 record was the best in the AFC Central. Though they lost in the
playoffs, it was a big step for a young team.

Paul Brown continued to show his football expertise by

> Cincinnati built the
> Bengals their first
> home, Riverfront
> Stadium. The team
> moved into the
> new Paul Brown
> Stadium in 2000.

Hall of Fame coach Paul Brown helped start the Bengals.

The Bengals switched uniform styles before the 1981 season. They added tiger stripes to their plain orange helmets and stripes to the shoulders of their black jerseys.

drafting a number of key players. In the coming years, they would help the team almost reach the top of the NFL. Quarterback Ken Anderson was drafted in 1971, and wide receiver Isaac Curtis in 1973. In 1973, these young stars helped the Bengals win their second division title.

Brown retired after the 1975 season, and the Bengals struggled for several years afterward. In 1980, however, they drafted a player who would become perhaps the best ever to wear the orange and black. Anthony Muñoz was an imposing offensive lineman from the University of Southern California. With Cincinnati, he proved to be the key to the team's powerful offense. Opening holes for running backs and protecting Anderson, Muñoz started a career that would eventually send him to the Hall of Fame.

Anthony Muñoz was a dominant tackle who was an All-Pro selection for 11 consecutive seasons from 1981 to 1991.

Powerful Anthony Muñoz is perhaps the best Bengals player ever.

Ken Anderson and the Bengals fought the Chargers and bitterly cold weather to reach Super Bowl XVI.

First, though, he helped the
Bengals reach the Super Bowl. In
1981, Anderson led the NFL in passing, Muñoz made his first Pro Bowl,
and Curtis was joined by Cris Collin-
sworth as key receivers. New coach
Forrest Gregg had played with cham-

pionship teams in Green Bay. He inspired the Bengals
to reach the AFC Championship Game, where they
faced an opponent tougher than anything in a
helmet: the weather. The game was played in Cincinnati in weather better for polar bears. The game-time
temperature was minus 11 degrees. **Windchill** made it
feel like almost minus 60! Yet the Bengals overcame
the terrible conditions to defeat San Diego 27–7.

In Super Bowl XVI, they lost to San Francisco,
but their conference title was the team's finest
moment to date.

The team made the playoffs again in 1982,
with Anderson setting an NFL record with a 70.55
completion percentage. The team struggled in the
next few seasons, but in 1988, the Bengals came
even closer to an NFL title. New quarterback Boomer
Esiason, a lefty, was the NFL's MVP. Helped by the
running back duo of James Brooks and Ickey Woods,
Cincinnati finished with an all-time best record
of 12–4. Woods became famous for his hopping,

Boomer Esiason passed for more career yards (37,920) than any other left-handed quarterback in NFL history.

skipping post-touchdown dance. "The Ickey Shuffle" caught the attention of fans around the country.

After defeating the Buffalo Bills to win the AFC title, Ickey and the Bengals shuffled off to the Super Bowl. In Super Bowl XXIII, the Bengals faced the mighty San Francisco 49ers, led by legendary quarterback Joe Montana. The Bengals stunned the NFC champs by taking a 13–6 lead into the fourth quarter. The 49ers tied the score at 13–13, but then Cincinnati kicker Jim Breech made his third field goal of the game with less than four minutes left. The Bengals led 16–13 with little time remaining.

However, Montana was famous for his last-minute winning drives. He led the 49ers downfield against a desperate Bengals defense. He completed a 10-yard touchdown pass to John Taylor with less than 34 seconds left to win the game. Once again, the Bengals were disappointed.

They would get used to that feeling in the next decade. From 1991 through 2002, the team never won more games than it lost in a season. The Bengals of recent years have had some fine players, including quarterback Jeff Blake and receiver Carl Pickens. Running back Corey Dillon is perhaps the best player the team has had since their Super Bowl days. In 2000, Dillon set an all-time NFL record with 278 yards in a single game. Bengals fans are hoping that the next part of this roller-coaster ride goes up!

Corey Dillon burst onto the national scene when he ran for 246 yards—at the time, the most by a rookie in NFL history—in a prime-time game in 1997.

The Bengals tried to hold on to the 49ers in Super Bowl XXIII, but lost in the final minute.

The addition of a new coach and top performers on offense gave
the Bengals' thrill ride a big boost. Quarterback Carson Palmer was
the first player chosen overall in the 2003 draft and took over the

Carson Palmer became the Bengals starting quarterback in 2004.

offensive reins the next season. Running back Rudi Johnson had a breakout season in 2004 with 1,454 yards and 12 touchdowns. Running the show was head coach Marvin Lewis, named to the job in 2003. He led the Bengals to two straight 8–8 seasons. For some teams, 8–8 would be disappointing, but for the Bengals, it was a sign that good things were ahead.

Marvin Lewis, who was hired as the Bengals' head coach in 2003, was the architect behind the Baltimore Ravens' record-setting defense in 2000.

In 2004, Rudi Johnson emerged as the Bengals' top running back.

THE CLEVELAND BROWNS

The Browns are the only NFL team that does not have any type of logo on their helmets.

The Cleveland Browns began their life in a league that was not part of the NFL. But in the more than 50 years since, they have made a lasting impact on the NFL in more ways than one. The team has won four NFL championships. It has also featured some of the game's greatest all-time players and the most vocal and loyal fans in the league.

Cleveland businessman Mickey McBride started the team in 1946 as part of a league called the All-America Football Conference (AAFC). He ran a contest in a newspaper to help pick a name for his new team. *Browns* won, in honor of their first coach. Paul Brown was not comfortable with having the team named after him, however. He suggested that perhaps it was a reference to boxing champion Joe Louis, who was known as the Brown Bomber. But no contest entries alluded to Louis.

Whether it was "his" team or not, Brown first made the Cleveland Browns a legendary team. The AAFC was around for only four seasons, and Cleveland won the championship every year. Brown

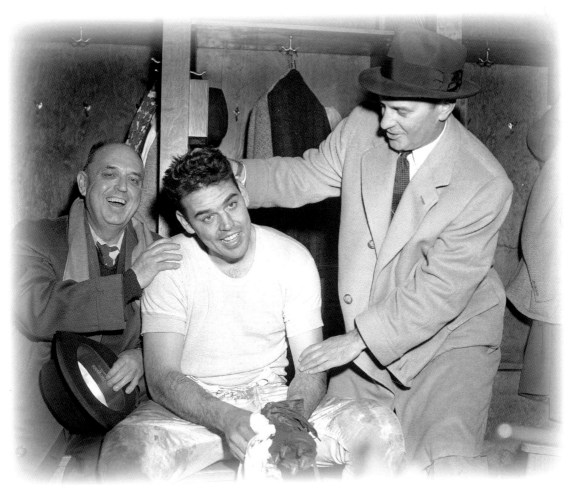

Otto Graham (center) celebrates another championship with his father (left) and coach Paul Brown.

brought many new developments to pro football. He was among the first coaches to study film of his opponents and to grade his players on their performance.

Brown also brought to the team some of the NFL's greatest all-time stars. Quarterback Otto Graham was a tough, solid player who did anything he needed to to make his team win. Graham led the Browns for 10 seasons, taking them to a title game every season.

The "taxi squad" started when original Browns owner Mickey McBride put players who were not on the active roster on the payroll of his taxicab company.

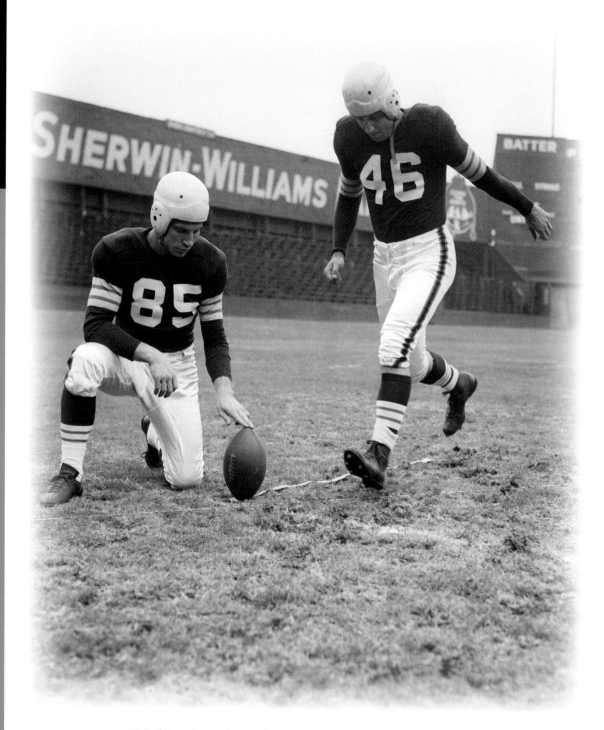

Hall of Fame lineman Lou "The Toe" Groza was also the Browns' kicker.

Running back Marion Motley was perhaps the hardest man to tackle in NFL history. Bill Willis and Lou Groza were Hall of Fame linemen.

It's important to note that in 1946, there were no African American players in the NFL. Yet Brown signed Willis and Motley to play for his AAFC team based on their skills, not the color of their skin.

Marion Motley was one of the toughest runners to tackle.

This touchdown by Otto Graham helped the Browns win the 1954 NFL title game.

The Browns and two other AAFC teams joined the NFL in 1950, and the older league challenged the new teams. They matched the Browns against the NFL-champion Philadelphia Eagles in the first game. The Browns stunned the NFL and the Eagles, winning easily 35–10. They continued to pound their NFL opponents all season, reaching the NFL Championship Game. Groza's 16-yard field goal with 28 seconds left gave the Browns the title over the Los Angeles Rams.

Though the Browns would reach the NFL title game in each of the next three seasons, they lost each game. In 1954, they made the big game again. Before it began, Graham announced that it would be his last. Inspired by their fearless leader, the Browns rolled to a 56–10 victory over the Lions. Graham had three touchdown passes and ran for three more scores. Brown eventually talked Graham into playing one more year, and the Browns won another title in 1955.

Two years later, another star joined the Browns. Running back Jim Brown (no relation

Powerful Jim Brown (32) was perhaps the NFL's best all-time running back.

In 1980, the Browns were known as the "Kardiac Kids." Thirteen of the team's 16 games were decided by a touchdown or less, often in the final moments of the game. They won 11 games that year.

to Paul Brown) was an All-American runner, lacrosse star, and track champion. He burst into the league in 1957, winning Rookie of the Year honors and leading the league in rushing yards. He dominated the league for almost a decade, winning a record eight NFL rushing titles.

New Browns owner Art Modell fired Coach Brown in 1962. In 1964, the new coach, Blanton Collier, relied on quarterback Frank Ryan and Jim

Brown to lead Cleveland to the NFL championship. It would be the last time the Browns would either play for or win the league title.

Cleveland went through some down years in the 1970s. In 1980, however, the team's loyal fans were rewarded with a trip to the AFC playoffs. Quarterback Brian Sipe led the NFL in passing and was the league MVP. But Sipe threw an interception in the end zone with less than a minute left, and the team lost the divisional playoffs. They were disappointed again when they lost back-to-back conference title games to Denver in 1986 and 1987. The Browns suffered another loss to the Broncos in 1989's AFC Championship Game.

Through it all, Cleveland fans were becoming famous around the league. Some fans in end-zone seats began wearing dog masks and throwing dog-bone cookies onto the field. "The Dawg Pound" remains the NFL's most well-known group of football fanatics.

But in 1995, those fans were stunned when Modell announced he was moving the team to Baltimore. It was a shock to a city that identified so closely with its team. The NFL promised to start another Browns team in the near future. That came in 1999, when a "new" Browns team was started from scratch. The Browns of today keep all of the old Browns records and colors and history. Unfortunately for the Dawg Pound, the "new" Browns have not yet matched the "old" Browns' record of success.

They did add to the team's winning legacy in 2002. Under the leadership of quarterback Tim Couch, who threw 18 touchdown passes, the Browns earned a wild-card playoff berth. They faced NFC

Lee Suggs led the Browns in rushing in 2004.

The new Browns won only 12 games from 1999 to 2001, but by 2002 had returned to the play-offs as a wild-card team.

North division rival Pittsburgh in the first round. It proved to be another disappointment. Cleveland led 24–7 and 33–21, only to watch Pittsburgh storm back over and over. A Steelers' score in the final minute ended the Browns' hopes, and Cleveland lost 36–33.

A bright spot since then was the play of running back Lee Suggs, who gained nearly 800 yards in 2004.

CHAPTER FOUR

THE PITTSBURGH STEELERS

T he Steelers are one of the NFL's oldest teams. For a long, long time, they were also one of the worst. But with a flurry of championships in the 1970s, they moved from the bottom to the top.

In 1933, Pennsylvania's government legalized sports events on Sundays. As soon as that happened, businessman Art Rooney bought the NFL franchise for Pittsburgh. He named his team the Pirates, after the local baseball team. After seven years without a winning record, the team changed its name to the Steelers in 1940. It didn't help; the Steelers still weren't very good.

During U.S. involvement in World War II (1941–1945), the entire NFL was smaller, as many of its players were in the armed forces in Europe or Asia. To keep playing in 1943, the Steelers merged with the Philadelphia Eagles and played one year as the "Steagles." In 1944, they mixed with the Chicago Cardinals as the "Card-Pitt Combine." After the war, the Steelers earned a playoff spot in 1947, but lost that game.

It was the last time they would be in the postseason for more

Art Rooney earned the money to buy the Steelers when he won a bet on a horse race.

The hybrid Steagles of 1943 did better than expected, going 5–4–1. But the Card-Pitt team of 1944 derisively was called the "Carpets" during an 0–10 season.

than two decades. The team was almost always on the bottom of the standings. To make matters worse, they cut future Hall of Fame quarterback Johnny Unitas in 1955. They decided not to draft Jim Brown, who also turned out to be a pretty good player.

In 1969, Rooney hired a new coach. Under Chuck Noll, the Steelers turned from doormats to champions. The key was Noll's ability to draft star

Art Rooney owned the Steelers for more than 60 years.

Hiring Chuck Noll was the smartest move Rooney ever made!

players. Each year, the NFL holds a selection draft. Teams choose college players to join their team. From 1969 to 1974, Noll and the Steelers chose nine players who would eventually land in the Hall of Fame. Along the way, those players helped the Steelers win four Super Bowls.

The Steelers are the only team to have a logo on only one side of their helmets—the right side.

"Mean" Joe Greene didn't get his nickname for his disposition. Instead, it was because he played college ball for the "Mean Green" at North Texas State.

The first piece of the puzzle was defensive tackle "Mean" Joe Greene, one of the best defensive players ever. Greene was soon joined by linebackers Jack Lambert and Jack Ham and cornerback Mel Blount. The Pittsburgh defense became known as the "Steel Curtain."

On offense, Noll chose quarterback Terry Bradshaw in 1970. A hard-throwing, wild-living kid from

Joe Greene became the heart of the "Steel Curtain" defense.

Tough and strong, Terry Bradshaw led Pittsburgh to four NFL titles.

With four touchdown passes, quarterback Terry Bradshaw (center) was the MVP of Super Bowl XIII.

Lynn Swann was inducted into the Pro Football Hall of Fame in 2001. One year later, John Stallworth—Swann's complement at wide receiver—made it in.

Louisiana, Bradshaw became an all-time great. He didn't start out that way, however. His first few seasons weren't very good. But Noll gave him some help with running back Franco Harris and receivers Lynn Swann and John Stallworth.

The team had a flash of its potential in 1972. The Steelers reached the playoffs for the first time since 1947. They played the Oakland Raiders and trailed late in the game, 7–6. Rooney was so sure the game was over, he took an elevator down to congratulate the Raiders. While he was going down, he missed one of the wildest plays in NFL history.

Bradshaw dropped back to pass and scrambled around, looking for a receiver. He spotted Frenchy Fuqua downfield and fired a pass. Fuqua, Oakland's Jack Tatum, and the football all arrived at the same spot at the same time. The ball ricocheted backward, and Harris, trailing the play, caught it at his shoe tops. While the Pittsburgh fans went wild and the Raiders gave chase, Harris romped the final 42 yards of the winning 60-yard touchdown. The play would forever be known as the "Immaculate Reception."

Two years later, the Steelers finally reached a title game, and they made the most of their chance. The Bradshaw-led offense and the Steel Curtain defeated Minnesota 16–6 in Super Bowl IX. Finally, after so many years of failure, Art Rooney owned an NFL champion.

The Steelers repeated their title in Super Bowl X, defeating Dallas. They won again in Super Bowl XIII after the 1978 season. In Super Bowl XIV, they wrapped up an amazing run of four championships in six seasons. They were the first team to win four Super Bowls (Dallas and San Francisco have since reached five wins apiece).

After the 1991 season and a couple more AFC Central Division titles, Noll retired. He was replaced by Bill Cowher, who would lead the team for the next decade and more.

In the 1990s, under Cowher, the Steelers were once again among the elite teams. They earned six playoff berths in the decade. The

Running back Rocky Bleier recovered from injuries suffered as a soldier in the Vietnam War to help the Steelers win four Super Bowls.

highlight was their 1995 AFC championship. Though they lost to Dallas in Super Bowl XXX, they showcased one of the league's most multitalented players. Kordell Stewart was a rookie on that team, and he became the team's regular quarterback in 1996. He was also a talented runner and caught several touchdown passes. He was nicknamed "Slash," because he was a quarterback/runner/receiver (get it?).

Slash's many talents helped the Steelers reach the AFC Championship Game after the 2001 season. Though they lost, it was a sign of good things to come for the Steel City.

Coming off a 6–10 season in 2003, the Steelers chose a big, strong-armed quarterback in the draft. It proved to be an inspired choice. Ben Roethlishberger took over as the starter in week 5 . . . and didn't lose for more than three months! He led the team to 13 straight victories, several of them in dramatic comebacks. This amazing rookie carried the team all the way back to the AFC Championship Game. They lost there to the defending Super Bowl-champion New England Patriots, but the young passer's spot on the field was assured.

Pittsburgh continues to feature a tough defense, while Art Rooney's son Dan now runs the team off the field. As the Steelers look to add to their championship legacy, Big Ben will lead the way on the field.

Ben Roethlisberger became the Steelers' leader as a rookie in 2004.

STAT STUFF

T E A M   R E C O R D S

TEAM	ALL-TIME RECORD	NFL TITLES (MOST RECENT)	NUMBER OF TIMES IN PLAYOFFS	TOP COACH (WINS)
Baltimore	72–71–1	1 (2000)	3	Brian Billick (61)
Cincinnati	242–321–1	0	7	Sam Wyche (64)
Cleveland	451–336–13	4 (1964)	24	Paul Brown (115)
Pittsburgh	479–465–20	4 (1979)	22	Chuck Noll (209)

M E M B E R S   O F   T H E   P R O   F O O T B A L L   H A L L   O F   F A M E

BALTIMORE PLAYER	POSITION	DATE INDUCTED
None		

CINCINNATI PLAYER	POSITION	DATE INDUCTED
Charlie Joiner	Wide Receiver	1996
Anthony Muñoz	Tackle	1998

MEMBERS OF THE PRO FOOTBALL HALL OF FAME

CLEVELAND

PLAYER	POSITION	DATE INDUCTED
Doug Atkins	Defensive End	1982
Jim Brown	Fullback	1971
Paul Brown	Coach	1967
Willie Davis	Defensive End	1981
Len Dawson	Quarterback	1987
Len Ford	Defensive End	1976
Frank Gatski	Center	1985
Otto Graham	Quarterback	1965
Lou Groza	Offensive Tackle/Kicker	1974
Henry Jordan	Defensive Tackle	1995
Leroy Kelly	Running Back	1994
Dante Lavelli	End	1975
Mike McCormack	Tackle	1984
Tommy McDonald	Wide Receiver	1998
Bobby Mitchell	Wide Receiver/Halfback	1983
Marion Motley	Fullback	1968
Ozzie Newsome	Tight End	1999
Paul Warfield	Wide Receiver	1983
Bill Willis	Middle Guard	1977

PITTSBURGH

PLAYER	POSITION	DATE INDUCTED
Bert Bell	Owner	1963
Mel Blount	Cornerback	1989
Terry Bradshaw	Quarterback	1989
Len Dawson	Quarterback	1987
Bill Dudley	Halfback	1966
Joe Greene	Defensive Tackle	1987
Jack Ham	Linebacker	1988
Franco Harris	Running Back	1990
Robert (Cal) Hubbard	Tackle	1963
John Henry Johnson	Fullback	1987
Walt Kiesling	Guard/Coach	1966
Jack Lambert	Linebacker	1990
Bobby Layne	Quarterback	1967
Johnny (Blood) McNally	Halfback	1963
Marion Motley	Fullback	1968
Chuck Noll	Coach	1993
Art Rooney	Owner	1964
Dan Rooney	Owner	2000
John Stallworth	Wide Receiver	2002
Ernie Stautner	Defensive Tackle	1969
Lynn Swann	Wide Receiver	2001
Mike Webster	Center	1997

MORE STAT STUFF

A F C   N O R T H   C A R E E R   L E A D E R S   (T H R O U G H   2 0 0 4)

BALTIMORE

CATEGORY	NAME (YEARS WITH TEAM)	TOTAL
Rushing yards	Jamal Lewis (2000–04)	5,763
Passing yards	Vinny Testaverde (1996–97)	7,148
Touchdown passes	Jamal Lewis (2000–04)	34
Receptions	Qadry Ismail (1999–2001)	191
Touchdowns	Jermaine Lewis (1996–2001)	22
Scoring	Matt Stover (1996–2004)	1,001

CINCINNATI

CATEGORY	NAME (YEARS WITH TEAM)	TOTAL
Rushing yards	Corey Dillon (1997–2003)	8,061
Passing yards	Ken Anderson (1971–1986)	32,838
Touchdown passes	Ken Anderson (1971–1986)	197
Receptions	Carl Pickens (1992–99)	530
Touchdowns	Pete Johnson (1977–1983)	70
Scoring	Jim Breech (1980–1992)	1,151

CLEVELAND

CATEGORY	NAME (YEARS WITH TEAM)	TOTAL
Rushing yards	Jim Brown (1957–1965)	12,312
Passing yards	Brian Sipe (1974–1983)	23,713
Touchdown passes	Brian Sipe (1974–1983)	154
Receptions	Ozzie Newsome (1978–1990)	662
Touchdowns	Jim Brown (1957–1965)	126
Scoring	Lou Groza (1950–59, 1961–67)	1,349

PITTSBURGH

CATEGORY	NAME (YEARS WITH TEAM)	TOTAL
Rushing yards	Franco Harris (1972–1983)	11,950
Passing yards	Terry Bradshaw (1970–1983)	27,989
Touchdown passes	Terry Bradshaw (1970–1983)	212
Receptions	John Stallworth (1974–1987)	537
Touchdowns	Franco Harris (1972–1983)	100
Scoring	Gary Anderson (1982–1994)	1,343

GLOSSARY

divisions—in the NFL, teams are placed in one of these four-team groups

interception—when a defensive player catches a pass thrown by the offense

lacrosse—a field sport in which players use long sticks with basket ends to throw and catch a ball; goals are scored by throwing the ball into a net

mascots—costumed characters that perform at sporting events

Pro Bowl—the NFL's annual all-star game, held in Honolulu, Hawaii

scrambled—when a quarterback runs around looking for an open receiver or makes a run past the line of scrimmage himself

selection draft—held each April, this is when NFL teams choose college players to join their teams; the teams with the worst records the prior year choose first, but draft picks can be traded to move a team's draft order

stable—lasting, not likely to change

Super Bowl—the NFL's annual championship game, played in late January or early February at a different stadium each year

windchill—a measurement of temperature that combines the air temperature with the wind speed

TIME LINE

1933 Pittsburgh Steelers founded

1946 Cleveland Browns founded as part of the All-America
Football Conference

1950 Cleveland joins the NFL and wins championship

1964 Cleveland wins another NFL title

1968 First season for the Cincinnati Bengals

1974 Pittsburgh wins Super Bowl IX, first of four Super Bowls it will
win in the next six seasons

1981 Cincinnati reaches Super Bowl XVI

1988 Cincinnati reaches Super Bowl XXIII

1995 Pittsburgh reaches Super Bowl XXX; Baltimore Ravens begin
play after moving from Cleveland

1999 "New" Cleveland Browns begin play

2000 Baltimore Ravens win Super Bowl XXXV

FOR MORE INFORMATION ABOUT

THE AFC NORTH AND THE NFL

BOOKS

Buckley, James Jr., and Jerry Rice. *America's Greatest Game.* New York: Hyperion Books for Children, 1998.

Gilbert, Sara. *The History of the Cleveland Browns.* Mankato, Minn.: Creative Education, 2005.

Nichols, John. *The History of the Baltimore Ravens.* Mankato, Minn.: Creative Education, 2005.

Smith, Ron (editor). *Cleveland Browns: The Official Illustrated History.* New York: McGraw-Hill, 1999.

Storybook Season: *The 2000 Baltimore Ravens' Run to the Super Bowl.* Baltimore: Baltimore Sun, 2001.

ON THE WEB

Visit our home page for lots of links about the AFC North:
http://www.childsworld.com/links

Note to Parents, Teachers, and Librarians: We routinely verify our Web links to make sure they are safe, active sites—so encourage your readers to check them out!

INDEX

A B O U T   T H E   A U T H O R

James Buckley Jr. has written more than 35 books on sports for young readers, including *Eyewitness Football* and *America's Greatest Game*, about NFL history. He was an editor at NFL Publishing and contributed to the league's magazines and the Super Bowl Program.